HOW TO BUY A
FRANCHISE
COLLECTION VOLUME 1

101 Questions To Ask
Before You Invest
In A Franchise

Dr. John P. Hayes
Your Personal Franchise Coach

7 DIRTY LITTLE
SECRETS OF
FRANCHISING

Protect Your
Franchise Investment

"He has spilled
all the beans in this
new eBook!"
J. Barry Watts,
Former Franchisee

DR. JOHN P. HAYES
YOUR PERSONAL FRANCHISE COACH

DR. JOHN P. HAYES
YOUR PERSONAL FRANCHISE COACH

7 Dirty Little Secrets of Franchising
Protect Your Franchise Investment

and

101 Questions to Ask
Before You Invest in a Franchise

Dr. John P. Hayes
HowToBuyAFranchise.com

E-Book Publication Date: 2017
ISBN: 978-0-9975536-5-9
Publisher: BizComPress
Copyright, 2017, John P. Hayes, Ph.D.

First edition published 2017
BizCom Press
A division of BizCom Associates
BizComPress.com
1400 Preston Rd #305, Plano, TX 75093

7 Dirty Little Secrets of Franchising was originally published as an e-book in 2015.

101 Questions to Ask Before You Invest in a Franchise was originally published as an e-book in 2013.

Read this Disclaimer

Please note: Neither this book, its author, or its publisher provide counsel or advice. This book and its contents are not intended for the purpose of buying a franchise. This book is a tool that might possibly be helpful in the process of evaluating a franchise business prior to investing in it. No one should invest in a franchise or any business based solely on the information in this book. Investing in a franchise is a serious matter that requires thorough investigation of the franchise opportunity, the franchisor, and related subjects. Franchising is not for everyone. The reader is advised to consult with a licensed professional for legal, financial and other professional services. The reader of this book assumes responsibility for the use of this information. The author and publisher assume no responsibility or liability whatsoever for the use or misuse of the information contained within this book.

How To Buy A Franchise Collection Volume I

7 Dirty Little Secrets of
Franchising
Protect Your Franchise Investment

and

101 Questions to Ask
Before
You Invest in a Franchise

Dr. John P. Hayes
HowToBuyAFranchise.com

CONTENTS

FOREWORD

Everyone appreciates a bargain, and so I decided to combine two of my best-selling titles into one book, as well as add some material that doesn't exist in either book.

As I've watched the sales of my books in recent years, I've noticed that many of the readers who bought *7 Dirty Little Secrets of Franchising*, originally published as an e-book in 2015, had also purchased *101 Questions to Ask Before You Invest in a Franchise*, my all-time best-selling franchise title, which was originally published as an e-book in 2013. Now, readers can buy both books in one, save money, and reap the bonus of the additional material.

But the real value goes beyond dollars and cents. If you're thinking about buying a franchise – and it seems almost everyone does at one time or another – you want to get accurate, truthful and insightful information just as fast as possible so that you can make an informed decision. And that's how this new title, *7 Dirty Little Secrets of Franchising and 101 Questions to Ask Before You Invest in a Franchise*, will help you.

In one sitting, you can read this book and either decide to pursue the acquisition of a franchise or not. If you decide that franchising isn't for you, you haven't invested much time or money. But if you decide that franchising is in your future, this is a book that you will return to time and again.

As you explore franchise opportunities, you'll come back to the book to be sure you avoid the "dirty little secrets." You'll also enjoy checking back to see which questions you should ask franchisors, franchisees, attorneys, accountants and others whom you meet in the process of buying a franchise.

The new material includes *17 Steps to Successfully Buying a Franchise,* a chapter that leads you through the process of finding, verifying, and ultimately acquiring a franchise. That section alone is worth the price of the book!

If you need money to acquire a franchise, then you'll find several solutions in *Funding Your Franchise Acquisition: Where Do You Get the Money?*

I wrote *Foreign Investors: Use Franchising to Get a U.S. Green Card* to explain the special visa program that helps people who want to move to the United States. And then I included a handy section called *Franchise Terms & Resources,* which you can use over and over to be sure you understand franchise jargon, as well as to consult reliable sources of information.

Whether you already know that you're going to buy a franchise, or you're just curious about the opportunity to become a franchisee, this book is a valuable resource. It also comes with my personal commitment to answer your questions about franchising. If, after reading this book, you still have questions, or you need clarifications, just ask me! My contact information is at HowToBuyAFranchise.com. And you don't need to worry that I'll try to sell you a franchise, because I don't sell franchises. My mission is to educate you about franchising and empower you so that you can decide whether or not you should buy a franchise.

That said, I invite you to read *7 Dirty Little Secrets of Franchising and 101 Questions to Ask Before You Invest in a Franchise.*

– Dr. John P. Hayes

INTRODUCTION

At any given moment, thousands of people across the world are thinking about buying a franchise business. Impressed by a business idea, or encouraged by a family member or friend, or possibly persuaded by a franchise broker, or dazzled by a franchise expo, a sizable percentage of these folks will buy a franchise opportunity with the hopes of achieving financial success, if not financial independence.

Good for them, except for those who will lose their money and may, in fact, ruin their lives financially and emotionally. Sadly, not all franchise investments turn out the way everyone involved had hoped at the time of signing the franchise agreement. Too many franchise investments go bottom-up. It doesn't need to end that way. Most times, in fact, it doesn't end that way. Even if the franchise investors don't become financially independent, or wildly wealthy, they achieve some degree of success, freeing themselves from jobs they hated, and building for themselves assets that they can one day sell.

So why do some franchise investments fail? Everyone involved in the process – the franchisor, the franchise advisors, the franchisor's sales representatives – want the best for the new franchisee, but sometimes that's just not enough. It's not enough for everyone to be forthcoming, or for everyone to do proper due diligence, or for everyone to admit that certain circumstances may not be exactly as they need to be, or as they appear, for the franchisee to succeed.

That said, I don't want you to reconsider your desire to buy a franchise, or your decision to buy one if you've already made it. Franchising is fabulously successful, and for most people, franchising is the only way they can succeed as business owners and operators. However, before you invest your money, which may indeed represent your life's savings, you need to grasp the fact that all franchise investments do not succeed. More of them could succeed if only the investor was better informed prior to the purchase.

And just to be sure that my position is clear, I believe that most franchisors are honest; they want their franchisees to succeed, and succeed beyond everyone's imagination. Think about what that success does for the franchisor's ability to sell more franchises and build brand-name value!

But at the same time, many franchisors, depending on the circumstances (e.g., how badly they need to sell a franchise), will intentionally withhold information that they are not legally required to divulge simply because they want to grow their network of franchisees. Of course, there are fraudulent franchisors who withhold information knowing full well that it will likely result in failure for their franchisees. In other cases, franchisors unintentionally withhold information that could make a difference in a franchisee's performance as a business owner and operator.

What to do? It's fairly simple. Before you buy a franchise, do your homework! Do the due diligence that's required. It's required of you! It's not the franchisor's responsibility to look out for your best interests. Even if a franchisor wanted to look out for your best interests, it's not possible. The franchisor will never know enough about you, and can't know for certain how you're going to perform as a franchisee until you become a franchisee. This is not about the franchisor!

American franchisors, in particular, are under intense scrutiny by regulators. They have been for years. They are required to comply with the most onerous franchise laws in any nation. They are required to disclose a couple dozen points of information about themselves and their businesses to help prospective franchisees make an informed investment decision.

As just one example, they are required to publicly reveal the names and contact information of their existing and former franchisees! Just think about the value of that information. As a prospective franchisee, you can get a list of existing franchisees, people who already made the decision to buy the franchise, and you can call them, visit them, and probe them for information to help you decide if investing in the franchise is a good idea. And yet, of the people who fail in a franchise, my guess is that most of them never contacted even one franchisee.

Maybe franchisors would help themselves by requiring franchisees to be interviewed by existing franchisees before selling a franchise (in fact, some do that). But again, this isn't about the franchisor. For the most part, franchisors are doing their part. You, as a prospective franchisee, must do your part. This is about you. You must protect yourself!

And, of course, you can.

In several of my books – *Buy "Hot" Franchises Without Getting Burned, Take the Fear Out of Franchising,* and *12 Amazing Franchise Opportunities* (See BooksByJohnHayes.com) – I've written extensively, with step-by-step instructions, about how to buy a franchise. Any one of those books will help you improve your odds of succeeding as a franchisee, master licensee, or regional developer.

But now, with *7 Dirty Little Secrets of Franchising*, I'm giving you another valuable tool that will enormously improve the value of your due diligence as you explore franchise opportunities. Yes, of course, there are secrets that franchisors don't want you to know.

In fact, since franchisors aren't legally required to discuss these issues, and since prospective franchisees rarely ever ask about these issues, it's just as easy to keep the secrets. In some cases, franchisors could argue that the information that was kept secret wasn't really all that pertinent to a prospect's decision to buy a franchise and had little effect on the franchisee's performance.

Well, maybe so. But if I'm investing my money, everything is pertinent. I want to explore the "dirty little secrets" and I'll decide for myself, perhaps in collaboration with my own advisors, if the information will negatively impact my future performance as a franchisee.

The only way to conduct that exploration is to know that these "dirty little secrets" exist, and then to probe the franchisor and franchisees to unravel the details. You now have before you a rare book that will give you the information and direction that you need to take your franchise due diligence to the next level.

Use the information wisely! Because, after all, if you're a good prospect for franchising – and you match yourself to an appropriate franchise business idea –

you're going to enjoy your business journey and achieve

the financial goals that you set out to claim. Franchising makes it possible . . . but you've got to make it work.

Dr. John P. Hayes
July 2015

7 DIRTY LITTLE SECRETS OF
FRANCHISING
Protect Your Franchise Investment

Dr. John P. Hayes
HowToBuyAFranchise.com

Before I tell you anything about the secrets of franchising, especially those that may be classified as "dirty little secrets," I want you to know that the majority of people engaged in franchising – especially as franchisors, franchise consultants, or representatives of franchisors, for example, franchise brokers – are not out to "get you" or anyone else. I make that claim based on nearly 40 years of real-world experience in franchising.

Franchising Is a Successful Methodology

For those who want to start and operate their own business, franchising works. But that isn't to say that franchising is a "get-rich-quick scheme," or "pie in the sky," or a "hypothetical phenomenon." The world has countless examples of successful franchising, both for franchisors and franchisees. It's not a gimmick. It's for real.

In addition, franchising is highly regulated, at least in America, so failing to disclose required information is a violation of U.S. federal laws, and in more than half a dozen instances, state laws. Franchisors face serious penalties for misconduct, and most franchisors and related parties take these matters seriously.

Therefore, if you invest the time to explore the pros and cons of franchising, your chances for success are not guaranteed, but they are better than average. You can never guarantee your success in any business, but with franchising, you *can* come close.

It's Up to You to Protect Your Interests

So if franchising is regulated in America (it's regulated in other countries, too, but not to the extent that it is in the U.S.), and franchisors take the laws seriously, why should you be concerned about the "dirty little secrets" of franchising?

Four reasons come to mind:

1. Even in a highly regulated environment, not everything that's important has to be disclosed. And even then, some things can be disclosed without being completely accurate.

2. Some people are greedy, including franchisors, franchise consultants, and franchise brokers. And greed is reason enough for people to hide information from you, particularly if they are not required to disclose it. Franchising is a fabulous model for distribution of products and services. But some people have discovered that it's also a fabulous way to use other people's money to build a business, grab the cash, and run. And for greedy people, that's too great of a risk to ignore.

3. You're not a citizen of the U.S. and/or you're buying a franchise to be operated outside of the U.S. Therefore, America's laws are not pertinent in your situation.

There may be other laws that govern the sale of a franchise to you as a non-American, but no laws are as onerous or as comprehensive as those of the U.S. when it comes to franchising.

4. Master franchising (i.e., buying the rights to develop a franchise brand within a territory or country) has become increasingly popular in recent years. But for many different reasons, disclosure to prospective master licensees is often sloppy and incomplete. Many of my readers live outside of the U.S. It's important that you know how to protect your interests.

5. Once again, I'm going to emphasize that most franchisors, franchise consultants, and franchise brokers are honest people. They don't want to take advantage of you, and they truly want to help you succeed in franchising. But you've got to protect yourself from those who don't see things that way.

When Franchisors Are Vulnerable, They Keep Secrets

Even honest people can keep information from you, especially if they want to make a sale. Sometimes, in fact, they don't know what they're not telling you that they should tell you, or they don't know that what they're telling you isn't totally accurate. At other times, they don't reveal information that they aren't required to reveal, even if it would help you, and especially not if it would discourage you. There are several sensitive areas of concern where franchisors are vulnerable, and depending on the circumstances, they may prefer to keep that information secret or simply not disclose it.

For these reasons, you must be constantly vigilant to protect yourself when you buy a franchise. It's not easy to identify the greedy people who want to take your money and run, but by asking probing questions, you can force the "dirty little secrets" to be revealed. If necessary, do the running yourself and keep your money in your pocket (or bank).

Ask Questions to Reveal Vulnerabilities & Avoid Secrets

Here are several sensitive topics that might lead to a franchisor keeping a "dirty little secret" . . . so be sure you probe in these areas.

#1. THE EFFECTIVENESS OF THE FRANCHISOR'S OPERATING SYSTEMS

Franchisors are not required to prove that their systems work or even exist. So they're not going to tell you if they need to improve their systems or create new systems. They'd rather keep that their secret.

Becoming the First Franchisee May Not Be an Advantage

It's not unusual for a new franchisor to begin selling franchises without fully developing or documenting the operating systems, which include marketing, training, customer service, customer acquisition, sales, etc. For one thing, it takes time and money to document these systems, and new franchisors will often delay the development of systems until they've sold some franchises and have some money. Therefore, even if the franchisor is willing to cut you a "great deal" (i.e., you pay half the regular franchise fee and no royalties for 12 months, etc.), you may not want to become a pioneer franchisee in a company that has not fully developed (and tested) its operating systems.

When you talk about the franchisor's operating systems, seek proof that they exist and work.

Ask these questions:

Have you documented how your business operates? Have you documented the customer acquisition system? The marketing system? The operations system? Other pertinent systems? . . . Ask to see the documents and to read sections of the documents. Ask to speak to franchisees who can back up the franchisor's promise that these systems actually produce favorable results.

How difficult is it to teach new franchisees what they need to know to operate the business successfully (i.e., profitably)? How challenging is it for new franchisees to learn how to operate the system? Once again, never take the franchisor's word for it when you can just as easily ask franchisees for proof. The franchisor may, in fact, have developed a dynamic system. The only problem is transferring the system to the franchisees. Maybe the system, or series of systems, is too complex. Or possibly, even though it looks good on paper, it doesn't work.

Does the business make money? Every month? Certain months? Only in certain circumstances (i.e., different climates, seasons, demographics, etc.)? Many franchisees will be willing to share their books with you and show you how cash flowed through their business.

#2. RATE OF TURNOVER IN THE FRANCHISE NETWORK

Franchisors are required to provide details about franchise termination, failures, and number of units sold, opened, and closed in the Franchise Disclosure Document (FDD). Again, the FDD is a U.S. regulation. Non-U.S. franchisors are usually not required to provide these details. And U.S. franchisors are not required to provide the details to non-U.S. citizens. However, if you're buying a franchise or a master license, or signing an agreement to become the development agent for a U.S. franchisor, be aware that the franchisor has an FDD, it's updated annually, and there's no reason why the franchisor should not share the FDD with you (unless the franchisor is protecting secrets). There's no law that says an FDD can't be shared with a non-U.S. citizen. Ask for it!

But even with an FDD in hand, unless you look carefully, or you ask the right questions, you may not get a clear picture of the franchise network's performance.

The Situation May Look Better Than It Is

In fact, it may appear as though every franchisee, or the vast majority of franchisees, succeed. None of the businesses close. There are few terminations. But you may not be getting the real picture.

Franchisors can buy their problems, thus the problems become secrets.

Legally! Even though the data about termination of franchises or the number of units closed was properly disclosed in the FDD, a franchisor may want to keep the details surrounding that data secret.

Is it possible the franchise network looks to be in a healthier position because the franchisor bought out failing franchisees to keep those units open and operating? The transfers (another word for "sales") were disclosed in the FDD, but if you knew the real circumstances, you would understand that those exiting franchisees were probably not successful and that's why they exited the network. That, and the fact that they ran out of money! Why weren't they successful? That would be important to know. In truth, there's some missing information here, but you probably would not know to ask for it.

Franchisors Disdain "Going Out of Business"

Franchisors never want to shutter their units. This is more of a problem for retail franchisors than service franchisors – when a home-based, mobile-based or office-based business fails and closes, not many people will know because the business doesn't have a storefront. It didn't even have a sign, so the public didn't know the location of the business. But an entire city population may know when a franchise on Main Street closes its doors for good. For the sake of continuity, to keep the doors open and the customers served, a franchisor may be willing to step in, buy out the franchisee, and keep the store open. Eventually the franchisor may re-sell the store to a new franchisee, but the circumstances behind the situation will never be revealed.

Ask these questions:

How many units/stores/locations are owned by the franchisor? It's not illegal for a franchisor to own stores, and franchisors are not required to own stores. Some franchisors own units for testing purposes, which may be an advantage to franchisees. You'd rather the franchisor experiment in its own unit rather than your unit, especially if the experiment fails.

Has the franchisor purchased any units from franchisees? If yes, probe for the circumstances behind those purchases. In fact, you have a right to ask for the name and contact information of franchisees who sold to the franchisor. Contact those franchisees for their side of the story. Sometimes these franchisees will not talk to you; sometimes they signed agreements with the franchisor that prohibit them from speaking about the circumstances relative to the sale. So ask the franchisor: *When you purchased these franchises from your former franchisees, did your contract include a provision that would prohibit the franchisees from talking about the circumstances of the sale?* That's not illegal, but it's also a good way to keep secrets secret.

How many franchisees transferred their businesses to new franchisees (or to the franchisor) and did so because they were failing financially? Don't ask that question of only the franchisor or your franchise broker. Ask franchisees! They know, and if you speak to enough of them, and you ask the question consistently, they will tell you.

#3. LAWSUITS FILED BY OR AGAINST THE FRANCHISOR

American franchisors are required to list their 10-year litigation history in Item 3 of the Franchise Disclosure Document (FDD). That document gives prospective franchisees a peek "under the covers" to see how the franchisor has behaved. Sadly, any franchisor with at least a dozen or so franchisees in America has probably been sued. It's important to keep in mind that many lawsuits are frivolous. Nonetheless, Item 3 is a good way to keep the bad franchisors in check.

What if you turn to Item 3 and there's a blank space? No lawsuits were filed by or against the franchisor. Or maybe just a few lawsuits that seem to be of little consequence. Does this mean the franchisor is honest and the franchisees are happy?

What's Percolating Doesn't Have To Be Disclosed

It could be a mistake to assume that everyone's happy in the franchise network, even when the franchisees aren't suing the franchisor and the franchisor isn't suing the franchisees. When disagreements occur in a franchise network and they cannot be resolved through meetings and discussions, the respective parties may notify their lawyers, but the next step may be arbitration. At any given time in any franchise network, there may be at least a couple of percolating legal issues, but that information does not have to be disclosed. The franchisor wants to keep disagreements a secret . . . and again, it's not illegal to do so.

Savvy franchisors, especially when they know they were wrong, will settle disputes before they get into an arbitrator's office or a courtroom. So this is another way for the franchisor to quietly pay for its sins without revealing secrets to prospective franchisees or the media.

How Are Rogue Franchisees Controlled?

Franchisees will also become more compliant when threatened by their franchisor. Franchisors are required to give errant franchisees notice to correct (or cure) a situation before termination, but, understandably, franchisors don't want to talk about the frequency of those notices, and legally they don't have to. They'd rather keep that information secret, even though it could reveal to you some key operational issues.

If cure notices relative to the same issue or issues are frequently sent to franchisees, someone needs to ask why. Why are franchisees struggling with these issues? Does training need to be improved? Is there something related to geography, territory, or location that's causing a problem? Are franchisees simply not able to comply?

Franchisees are often bound by their agreements with franchisors to keep these matters confidential. They're also often required never to say anything negative about their brand, or company, because it could tarnish the franchisor's image and ability to sell franchises. In turn, that could hurt the business of other franchisees. These are not illegal requirements, but not knowing key points of information may be a disadvantage to you as a prospective franchisee.

Ask these questions:

How often, in the last 24 months, has the franchisor issued correction notices (or notices to cure) to franchisees? If you have the opportunity (and you can ask for it), put that question to the franchisor's in-house attorney or legal advisor. *What was the nature of those notices? Why were they issued?*

Does the franchise network include a franchisee advisory council? If so, what operational issues have been raised by the council? Where do the council and the franchisor not see eye to eye? Ask: *Who serves on the council? How do I speak to franchisees on the council?*

Are franchisees threatening to file a lawsuit against the franchisor? If so, for what reason? In America, threats of lawsuits are not uncommon and franchisors are not easily intimidated by these threats, especially if their franchise contract requires franchisees to seek arbitration. Franchisors might easily assume that somewhere in their franchise network, especially with 50 or more franchisees, someone is unhappy and may be willing to take legal action. But for the most part, franchisors will not own up to these threats. On the other hand, if you speak to enough franchisees, you're likely to find out if legal problems are brewing. Even if they are, that doesn't mean the franchisees are right and the franchisor is wrong. But you're better off knowing these issues before you buy the franchise than to discover them after you buy the franchise.

#4. IMPLEMENTATION OF THE NON-COMPETE CLAUSE

One of the ironies of franchising is that early in the franchisor/ franchisee relationship, the franchisee hangs on the franchisor's every word. But once the franchisee masters the business (or thinks he or she has) and knows how to generate a profit, he or she often wants to separate from the franchisor.

Suddenly the franchisee says to the franchisor, "I don't need you any more." In translation that means: "I don't want to pay fees to you anymore!"

Franchisees will justify this by saying, "Now that I've learned how to operate the business, I rarely need to tap into the franchisor's resources. I don't need the training department. I don't call the support staff. In fact, unless it's an unusual problem, I never call the franchisor anymore. They call me for assistance more than I call them. For example, they like me to talk to prospective franchisees to validate the system and help them sell franchises. So what am I paying for?"

But keep this in mind. No franchise contract says that you have to pay fees only until you learn the business. Franchise fees are forever! Franchisors recognize that, early in the franchisor/franchisee relationship, there may be little to no profit for the franchisor. During those years, the franchisee clings on to the franchisor's resources, including the training and support team, and may call the franchisor every day. The franchisor may travel to visit the franchisee to help get the business profitable. The franchisor spends money to help the franchisee learn the business and turn a profit. The franchisor makes this investment, or endures little to no profit, believing that eventually the franchisee will master the business and the franchisee's consistent royalty payments will make up for those lean years.

Besides all that, franchisors aren't so generous that they're willing to teach people how to master their business only to let those people compete with them. Come on. First and foremost, franchising is a business. *That's* not a secret!

Can You Compete With the Franchisor, Legally?

Franchisors include a non-compete clause in their franchise contracts to discourage competitors. By contract, a franchisee may be prohibited from operating the same business, or a similar business, separate from the franchisor for a period of two or more years. The specific circumstances vary from state to state.

The secret is that the non-compete requirement may not be legal, or it's not enforceable. Franchise agreements are enforced within specific states, and many states make it difficult to enforce non-compete clauses. But the franchisor doesn't want you to know that. Franchisors also don't want you to know that this is a clause that they will agree to "negotiate" if not delete from the contract. Few franchisors would allow a non-compete to get in the way of a franchise sale.

Ask these questions:

Is there a non-compete clause in the contract? If the answer is yes, and you find that offensive or problematic, ask the franchisor to delete it. Be prepared for the franchisor to say no. Or instead of a two-year non-compete, ask for a one-year.

Has the franchisor ever enforced a non-compete clause when a franchisee left the business and continued to operate a similar business? If yes, get specific information. Find out the name and location of the operator, who may still be in business. If so, contact that operator.

What is the opinion of the state (where you reside and will operate the franchise) regarding non-compete clauses? Call the attorney's general office in your state and ask for an explanation.

#5. TERMS THAT CONTROL THE RENEWAL OF THE FRANCHISE

It's important to pay attention to the renewal details in your franchise agreement. You may need to probe for certain information relative to the renewal of your franchise.

Franchise agreements are usually time-based. Typically, a franchisor grants a franchise license for five to 10 years. No secrets there.

Do You Want Your Franchise on Auto-Renewal?

However, at the end of the contract, the franchise may be automatically renewed at the then-"current terms," meaning that your royalty fee, and other fees, were automatically increased. Now, if you read your contract in advance, you would be aware of this clause, but in the excitement of getting a new business off the ground, it's easy to overlook details relative to a renewal that may be five to ten years away. And on the chance that those details might discourage you from buying the franchise, the franchisor or the franchise broker may purposely *not* discuss the details with you. That's simply good salesmanship.

You also should be aware that your franchise won't be renewed unless you trigger the renewal. If you're not aware that pulling the trigger is your responsibility (i.e., 60 days before the end of your current contract you must inform the franchisor in writing that you intend to renew). Or if you legitimately forgot to pull the trigger, the franchisor isn't obligated to overlook the facts at hand and renew your franchise. The franchisor also wasn't obligated to remind you to pull the trigger!

At the time of the initial sale, the franchisor intended to renew your contract – franchisors usually want to keep their franchisees rather than endure the cost of replacing them. However, if you turned out to be a rogue franchisee – a disgruntled franchisee, a lazy franchisee, a disagreeable franchisee, etc., or a franchisee who didn't pay any or much royalties – the franchisor will be looking for a way to remove you from the franchise network. Non-renewal is an easy way to do that.

None of these scenarios may please you, so be careful.

More importantly, especially if you want to renew your contract and the franchisor wants you to as well, be aware that you are in the catbird seat! Now is your opportunity to negotiate, but don't expect the franchisor to tell you that.

For example, upon fulfillment of your current contract, the contract automatically renews for another 10 years, thus obligating you for 10 more years. But look at the new terms. For the first 10 years, you paid a 5 percent royalty to the franchisor, a 2 percent royalty to the Franchise Marketing Fund, and $2,900 a year for training.

The new terms reduced the training requirement to $1,900 a year (because a seasoned franchisee should not require as much training) but increased the royalties to 8.5 percent and 3 percent, respectively. The franchisor now requires you to attend the annual convention or pay a $1,000 penalty fee.

In most cases, the renewing franchisees will go along with

the then- "current terms," but you don't have to, especially if you're a valued franchisee. If you've been paying your fees as required, you've learned the business, you've contributed to the franchise network, and you're considered by the franchisor and other franchisees as an asset to the franchise network, speak up. Negotiate your renewal. The franchisor will willingly negotiate with you, but they'd rather keep that a secret.

Can You Live With the New Terms?

Should your franchise automatically renew by the then-"current terms," you need to take a look at the circumstances and understand what the new terms will mean for your future.

For example, in the last five years that you were a franchisee, the demographics of your protected territory changed, and not in your favor. You have fewer customers (because the population of your territory is declining) and your customers are spending less money (because there's been a recession). Can you afford to operate the business for the next 10 years with the "current terms"?

Granted, you can't be obligated to this new contract without accepting it and signing it, but unless you're well aware of the details in advance, you may feel rushed to make a decision. This is a good time for you to know that you can request an extension from the franchisor – ask the franchisor, in writing, to extend your existing contract (and terms) by 180 days (or more). Usually, the franchisor will give you an extension, but it might be only a matter of weeks or a couple of months. Even so, the extra time gives you the opportunity to consider your future in the franchise and decide what to do. It might be time to sell your franchise.

There's nothing wrong with selling a franchise; it's an opportunity

Often times, franchisees want to sell rather than renew their franchises. Selling a franchise is not a negative. Thousands of happily retired (and wealthy) folks are former franchisees – but they didn't sell because they had to; they sold because it was their choice to sell.

Franchise resales are very desirable by people who are not interested in, or not cut out for, a startup business. Some people would rather pay a higher fee for an existing business than to have to start a business from scratch. Nothing wrong with selling a franchise; it's an opportunity to cash out on years of hard work.

You have the right to sell your franchise whenever you want, and you'd like it to be on your terms. Actually, a good franchisor wants the sale to be on your terms, too. You don't want to be forced into selling. So be careful. It's important to understand the terms relative to renewal, transfer (which means to sell), and termination of your franchise license.

And keep this in mind: The franchisor is not obligated to find a buyer for your franchise, and you do not have the right to sell your franchise to anyone without the franchisor's consent. Those details are in your franchise contract. Other terms in the contract dictate how a transfer (sale) will be handled. Upon the sale, you may owe certain fees to the franchisor or be responsible for commissions for the sale. Read the fine print! And negotiate before you commit to the franchisor.

Ask these questions:

How often do franchisees not renew their contracts? Probe further: *Why do franchisees not renew?* The FDD, by law, must include the names and contact information for previous franchisees. See if you can contact a few of those individuals to gather more details.

What's the franchisor's system for initiating the renewal process and negotiating the new terms with an existing franchisee? Ask franchisees that question! Find a franchisee who recently renewed his or her agreement and ask how the process occurred.

What support does the franchisor provide to a franchisee who wants to sell either at the end of the contract or before the contract expires? Keep in mind that franchisors sometimes (but rarely) want to buy locations from franchisees. Or they may know of existing franchisees who want to buy additional units.

On the other hand, the franchisor may not be very cooperative in helping you sell your franchise because the franchisor stands to gain more financially (at least at the outset) by selling a new franchise. Also, the franchisor doesn't want to get caught up in your sale – if you misrepresent details related to your franchise (even franchisees have secrets!), the franchisor doesn't want to be accused of colluding with you. After all, once you're out of the network and your buyer is in the network, the franchisor wants to develop a good working relationship with your replacement. Don't despair on this issue—business brokers sell existing franchises and will be pleased to help you, providing you have a profitable business to sell.

#6. TERMS THAT CONTROL THE TERMINATION OF THE CONTRACT

Some years ago I knew a franchisee who had decided to terminate his contract three years before the contract was to expire. He wasn't going to sell his franchise because he had never turned a profit and he really had nothing to sell. In the process of termination, the franchisor sent him an invoice for a large amount of money. When he asked the franchisor for an explanation, he was told that the amount represented the money he would have paid to the franchisor had he continued as a franchisee and paid at least the minimum fees.

"But I'm not continuing as a franchisee," the franchisee argued. "I'm closing my business."

Here's Money You Didn't Realize You Would Owe

The franchisor responded, "We understand. However, you signed a contract promising to pay us a certain amount of money annually for five years. It's only been two years. We are demanding the money due for the remaining three years."

The franchisee had signed a personal guarantee. So had his spouse.

Double ouch.

If You Don't Ask, the Franchisor Won't Tell

Was the franchisor legally right? Yes. But the franchisee clearly didn't understand the ramifications of terminating his contract before the contract ended. And the franchisor kept those ramifications secret until it was necessary to disclose them. And again, that's not illegal. In a sales transaction, good salespeople know not to bring up points that could squash the sale.

Ask these questions:

What are the ramifications if a franchisee wants to sell his/her franchise before the contract ends?

What terms can be negotiated that would minimize the ramifications of selling a franchise before the contract ends? For example, do you have to sign a personal guarantee? Does your spouse? Ask the franchisor to remove these requirements. Many will because they want to sell you a franchise!

How often do franchisees succeed by re-selling their franchises? Is there a market for re-sales?

#7. NECESSARY PERSONAL QUALITIES THAT LEAD TO SUCCESS IN THIS FRANCHISE

Many franchisors do not understand that their franchisees are their customers. They think their customers are the retail customers who buy their products or services. Of course they are, but the franchisor's primary customer is the franchisee – the person who paid possibly thousands of dollars to become a franchisee and promised to pay, over a period of time, thousands of dollars more in royalties and fees. Sadly, many franchisors don't recognize that these terms create a customer relationship.

Franchisors Should Invest in Franchisees

Consequently, these franchisors don't think much about how their customers feel at any given time, and they don't invest money to keep their customers. It's not unusual for a franchise network to lose 10 percent or more of its customer (franchisee) base every year. The franchisor must disclose information about system-wide turnover, but unless you know what you're looking for, it's not easy to get a true picture of a franchisor's turnover. There are ways to disguise turnover – for example, buying out failing franchisees, as stated earlier in this report. You will rarely find a franchisor disclosing a percentage of turnover. Unless they're proud of it, they keep that information as secret as possible. Even if the franchisor discloses the percentage of turnover, you may not want to trust it because turnover can be disguised – legally.

Turnover is a result of many factors, including disagreements between franchisor and franchisee, personality clashes, faulty systems, failure to perform (by either the franchisor or franchisee), etc. Sometimes turnover is inevitable because the franchisor selected the wrong franchisee (which is a failure of the franchisor's sales system).

Many franchisors claim that they can train almost anyone who's trainable to succeed in their franchise.

Franchising Is Not for Everyone

But it's not true. Franchising is not for everyone. And not every franchise opportunity works for every franchisee. Franchisors make these claims because they want to sell franchises and, in some cases, they must sell franchises to meet their monthly overhead, including payroll.

Some retail franchisees would not succeed in service businesses, and vice versa. But the issue is even deeper than that: Some people will not succeed in any kind of franchise opportunity, period. Not only are they not trainable, they're just not good franchisee prospects. Oftentimes, they lack the personality, the skills, and the behaviors to succeed in a franchise.

It's Different Strokes for Different Folks!

But even good franchise prospects (i.e., those who are trainable) with the right personality, skills and behaviors, will not perform equally in different franchises. Depending on the requirements of the franchise opportunity, some people will perform better or worse than others.

I strongly believe in matching a person's abilities to the needs of the franchise opportunity.

If the franchise opportunity requires a franchisee who's capable of selling products and services, the franchisee had better be good at selling.

- If the franchise opportunity requires a franchisee who is nurturing for the sake of capturing and keeping customers, the franchisee better be good at nurturing.

- If the franchise opportunity requires a franchisee who can influence people, the franchisee better be influential.

- If the franchise opportunity requires a franchisee who upholds high standards for quality and performance, the franchisee better be competent.

- Every franchise opportunity requires different skills and behaviors. Therefore, not everyone can succeed in every franchise opportunity. The savvy franchisor knows which skills and behaviors are needed and then awards or sells franchise licenses to people who possess those skills and behaviors.

Does the Franchisor Even Know Who Succeeds in the Business?

Not all franchisors believe in this principle, however. They will tell you that if you're trainable or teachable and you're cooperative, they can show you how to succeed in their business.

Don't believe it!

These franchisors may not even know why their most successful franchisees are successful. They may not be able to separate influential franchisees from nurturing franchisees, for example. And that's a mistake. They've never looked at their franchisees in terms of which ones are most valuable to them, that is, which franchisees pay them the most money while also following the franchisor's systems.

These franchisors do not know their most successful franchisees because they don't know why franchisees succeed. They've not invested the time to match skills and behaviors to franchisees . . . if they did so, they would discover that the franchisees who pay the least in royalties have similar personalities.

Some franchisors know which skills and behaviors that franchisees need to succeed in their business. Even if a prospective franchisee doesn't possess those attributes, the franchisor will make the sale anyway. Hiding specific skills and behavior requirements is a "dirty little secret" because disclosing that information would kill the sale. And, sadly, that disclosure is not required.

As a protective device, many franchisors will not use personality profiling because they believe they can't be held responsible for what they didn't know about their franchisees.

Franchisors may rationalize, "Well, our franchisees learn the skills that are necessary to operate our business in our world-class training program and by consulting with our world-class support team."

Don't believe that, either!

Or if you do, ask for a guarantee in writing.

What if a skill that you don't possess can't be learned? Or

what if you can't learn a behavior well enough to be profitable in your new franchise business? Or what if the business requires a skill that makes you uncomfortable? Or goes against your personal creed? Not everyone wants to sell products or services; not everyone cares to be nurturing; not everyone wants to be influential; not everyone wants to worry about quality and standards. But if the franchise you buy requires skills and behaviors that you don't possess (and possibly don't care to possess), you're at a huge disadvantage and may likely lose your investment.

To repeat: The skills and behaviors required to operate a franchise profitably do not have to be disclosed.

What can you do? First, ask all the important questions before you invest in a franchise. I've listed most of these questions – and indicated to whom you should present the questions – in 101 Questions to Ask Before You Invest in a Franchise, an Amazon.com best seller for many years.

Then, match yourself to the franchise opportunity. You can begin to do that by completing a DISC Profile. Use this free link:

surveymonkey.com/r/howtobuyafranchise.

The information you can glean from a DISC Profile is important for you to know about yourself, and you can share it with franchisors, franchise consultants and franchise brokers, whom you may have asked to help you find a franchise to buy.

A DISC Profile won't tell you which franchise to buy, but it will give you clear indicators so that you'll know the type of franchise business that makes sense for you. In other words, the kind of business that's compatible with your values, skills, behaviors and overall personality. When you use the link I provided above, I'll send you information that explains your DISC Profile and how it relates to franchising.

Ask these questions:

What type of person adapts most successfully to the franchisor's systems? Probe further by asking about gender, age, religion, previous experience, education, etc.

What skill sets do your top (best-performing) franchisees possess?

What skill sets are your bottom (lowest-performing) franchisees missing?

To me, few things are more important than matching the person to the franchise. Knowing yourself, knowing your values, skills, behaviors, and overall personality, and looking for those same qualities in a franchisor's operating system, is the best way to protect yourself when you buy a franchise. Unfortunately, most franchisors do not recognize the importance of this exercise – and, in fact, they may disagree with me.

IN CONCLUSION

And now you know the 7 *Dirty Little Secrets of Franchising*, and better yet, you know how to protect yourself from them. Whether you're buying one unit, multiple units, or a master license to develop a network of franchise units in a foreign territory or country, there's much you can do to protect yourself before buying a franchise.

Most people in franchising are honest. Most franchisors, franchise brokers and franchise consultants, want you to succeed. But when it's a matter of closing a sale, or sharing information with you that might kill the deal, even some of the best-intentioned people may keep secrets from you.

There are no guarantees in franchising, so you must make it a point to protect yourself. And now you know how!

101 QUESTIONS TO ASK
BEFORE
YOU INVEST IN A FRANCHISE

Dr. John P. Hayes
HowToBuyAFranchise.com

HOW TO USE THIS LIST

After buying a house, buying a franchise may be your largest investment ever, and it's not something that should be done without a great deal of questioning. Even then, *most people shouldn't do it at all.*

For more than 30 years, I've told people that *franchising may be the safest way to go into business, but it's not for everyone, and it may not be for you.* Sadly, people buy franchises for many of the wrong reasons. They buy them because they want to replace a job, or because someone (perhaps a parent, spouse or best friend) told them they'd make a great franchisee, or because a salesperson twisted their arm (yes, of course that still happens).

Is franchising for you?

The worst-case scenario: People who buy franchises without doing the required homework, which, when you think about it, essentially boils down to asking a lot of questions. If you spend several weeks asking questions about franchising, and especially about a specific franchise that you want to buy, you are likely to figure out if it's a good investment for you.

Of course, if you don't know *what* to ask – and, more importantly, *who* to ask – you're at a disadvantage, and you may not do your homework. Or you might do your franchise

homework the way I used to do my high school homework
– "*not very well,*" according to most of my teachers. You can
get away with "*not very well*" in high school, but you probably
won't when you invest six figures or more in the wrong
business opportunity.

At a minimum, when you buy a franchise, you must
ask questions of the franchisor, franchisees, professional
advisors (including a franchise attorney and a franchise-wise
accountant), and others. And now, knowing *what* to ask isn't
an issue because I'm about to give you the key questions
to ask. Knowing *who* to ask isn't a problem, either, because
I'm about to tell you who to ask. And while my list cannot
possibly include *every* question you should ask, it at least gives
you a good start, and sometimes that's the momentum you
need to do your homework "*better than good,*" as the late Zig
Ziglar used to say.

Real experiences led to these questions

I first created this list of questions many years ago to help
the franchise prospects whom I coach. Through the years, I've
refined the list by adding and combining questions. Most of
these questions are based on my experiences teaching people
about franchising . . . but, more importantly, many of the
questions are based on my personal experiences as a franchisee
(of several different concepts), a franchisor (leading more
than 265 franchisees), and an advisor to dozens of franchise
companies, public and private, domestic and international.

Track the answers

My recommendation is that you ask most of the questions
on this list and other questions that will arise during your
franchise exploration. I also recommend that you keep track

of the answers to all of the questions you ask. It's best to create a spreadsheet that includes the questions you asked, who you asked, and the respective answers. That way, after you've asked questions of a dozen or perhaps several dozen people, your spreadsheet results will help you in your final analysis of franchising, as well as specific franchise concepts. When you finally reach the end of your exploration and ask the definitive question, "Do I or do I not buy this franchise?" your answer will shout out at you from the spreadsheet.

Answers to many of the questions, especially those that inquire about franchising in general, can be found in books and magazines, and from a variety of online sources.

I've also included answers in my e-book, *Buy "Hot" Franchises Without Getting Burned, A Checklist for Your Franchising Success,* which you can purchase at *amazon. com/dp/B00EPFSXV4/.* You may also consult the International Franchise Association, franchise.org, the International Franchise Expo, IFEinfo.com, or numerous other credible sources, including the U.S. Small Business Administration, SBA.gov.

Questions that are specifically about a franchise company must be answered by the franchisor of that company, its franchisees, and related sources. You may also learn about specific companies, or specific details related to companies, through your professional advisors, including lawyers, accountants, leasing agents, bankers, and franchise advisors.

Ask the "me" questions

Some of the most important answers can only come from *you.* Buying a franchise is a personal experience, and yet most people don't seem to treat it that way.

People like to buy what's "hot," even though that's the

47

fastest way to get burned. Or people will buy a franchise because they know someone who bought the same franchise and that someone is making a lot of money. What people don't understand is that even if franchising works for two people, those two people will not necessarily succeed equally in the same franchise concept. Why? Because people are different. The franchise may not be different, but if the requirements of the franchise do not meet the unique skills and preferences of a franchisee, failure is likely to be the result.

Even many franchisors scratch their heads and say, "I don't understand why he failed." He, whoever he is, failed because he was not a good fit for the business. Had *he* understood the skill requirements of the franchise business and the expectations of the franchisor, and then objectively assessed his expectations and abilities, *he* would likely have known to buy another franchise, or maybe no franchise at all.

Unfortunately, because people get in a rush to buy a franchise – it's a very emotional experience – they do not ask the all-important *me* questions. And, sad to say, many franchisors do not require their prospects to ask those questions.

Assess your compatibility with franchising

It's critically important to know if you're a fit for franchising, and not just franchising but a specific franchise business. You may be great in a fast-food business but horrible in a service business – much depends on your skills and expectations.

You can learn more about your compatibility with franchising in general, and with specific franchises, by completing a DISC Profile. Use this free link: surveymonkey.com/r/howtobuyafranchise.

After you complete the profile, I'll follow up with information that you can share with franchisors, franchise brokers, and others who may be helping you discover appropriate franchises to buy. Some franchisors will insist that you complete a personality profile prior to selling you a franchise. Unfortunately, this isn't a universal requirement.

Unless you've got a lot of money, and/or you're a savvy business operator, you should get answers to the majority of the questions listed below. Furthermore, you should make certain you understand and agree with the answers to the questions on this list before you invest money in a franchise.

Ready to begin your franchise exploration? Here are key questions to ask, as well as whom to ask!

QUESTIONS ABOUT FRANCHISING IN GENERAL . . .

You can get answers to these questions from a variety of sources, including books and periodicals, library resources, and franchise experts. Just be sure the sources you use are objective and reliable!

1. What *is* franchising, how does it work, why does it work, and why doesn't it work?

2. What are the franchise disclosure document and the franchise agreement, and how do I get these documents?

3. What is a franchise fee? Why is it necessary? What does it pay for and how does it benefit the franchisee?

4. What is a franchise royalty fee, how much does it cost, when is it paid, and how does it benefit the franchisee?

5. If I want out of the franchise, can I sell it? Under what circumstances?

6. Are there any guarantees for me as a franchisee? If so, what are they?

7. Why do some franchisees succeed and others fail?

8. If I sell the franchise, can I continue to work in the same industry?

QUESTIONS ABOUT YOUR ABILITY TO BECOME A SUCCESSFUL FRANCHISEE . . .

For most of these questions, you'll rely on yourself for the answers. However, people who know you well and are not afraid to give you objective feedback can also provide helpful answers. For some questions, you may want to contact an advisor to help you think through all the related issues.

9. Why do I think I'm a good fit for franchising? Why will it work for me? Do I know that my personality is a good fit for franchising in general and for specific kinds of franchises (i.e., retail, service, food, etc.)?

10. How much money can I comfortably afford to invest in a franchise?

11. Do I like following a system or would I really prefer to create my own system?

12. Am I a good manager? Do I want to employ and manage people?

13. How long could I survive in a business without getting a paycheck?

14. Would my family support me if I become a franchisee?

15. Would investors support me (i.e., invest in me) as a franchisee? If I had to borrow money to invest in a franchise, where would I borrow it?

16. Do I like to market and sell?

17. Do I like serving people, including people who can be "ugly" customers?

18. What kinds of businesses interest me? What products would I like to sell, or what services would I like to represent? Am I a customer of any franchises that interest me?

19. If I were a businessperson, what could I do better than someone else?

20. What scares me about becoming a franchisee?

21. Who could I consult with about becoming a franchisee?

22. Can I earn more money as a franchisee than I can as an employee?

QUESTIONS ABOUT FRANCHISE OPPORTUNITIES . . .

Earlier questions focused on franchising in general and "matching" yourself to franchising. Now you're looking at specific franchise opportunities and you'll need to get answers from franchisors, franchisees, and disclosure documents.

23. What are the common features of these franchises? Why am I attracted to this type of franchise opportunity or brand?

24. What's not right (if anything), or what makes me uneasy, about these franchise opportunities?

25. Why would I invest in these franchises as opposed to starting a similar business myself?

26. What does the founder or president of each of these franchise opportunities say about the company's future? Do I agree with what he/she says?

27. How much is the franchise fee? How does one franchisor's fee compare to competitive franchisors? Is the fee refundable? What does it include? Do franchisees agree that the fee is reasonable?

28. How much training do I get when I invest in the franchise? Do I think I'll need more training? If so, where would I get it? How good is the training the franchisor

provides? Do most franchisees say the training is worth the investment? Who conducts the training classes – one person or multiple people? What are the trainer's qualifications? Where is the training conducted? For how long? Do I have to pay for the training?

29. After I become a franchisee, who will I communicate with at the franchisor's headquarters? Do I think I can work with this person?

30. After I become a franchisee, what kind of support will I get? Do the franchisees say the franchisor's support is effective? Do I have to pay for any of the support? How is the support provided? By phone? In person? By Internet?

31. If I have a question that I can't answer while a customer is standing in front of me in my business, how difficult will it be to reach the franchisor to get a quick response?

32. Do I get an operations manual? Do the franchisees say it's valuable? How often is it updated? Are the updates available online?

33. How good are the company's products? How good are the company's services? What do franchisees and customers say about the quality of the company's products and services?

34. Where is the company headed in the next five to 10 years? New products? New training and support programs?

35. How confident do I feel about the leadership of the franchise company?

36. How confident do I feel about the training and support staff of the franchise company?

37. What do the media say about the franchise company?

Any negative articles or reports about the franchisor? Franchisees? Products/services?

38. Have franchisees or customers commented online about the franchisor, franchisees, the product/service, the brand?

39. Who's responsible for advertising and promoting the company's products and services? Is there a national advertising fund? If so, how much do the franchisees contribute to the fund? How is that money used? How will the fund help me build my business?

40. If I need a physical location to operate the business (i.e., in a strip center, at a mall, or a dedicated building), do I have to find and select it myself? If so, do I know how to do that? What help will the franchisor provide? How good is the franchisor's track record at selecting locations? What are the criteria for selecting a location?

41. If I need to purchase products from the company, how fast will my orders be fulfilled? How will they be fulfilled? How will they be delivered to me? Could I purchase the same products for less money elsewhere?

42. Do I have the right (educational or professional) background to become a franchisee with this company? How do I compare to other franchisees who are successful?

43. Can I see myself operating this business for the next 10 to 30 years?

44. Am I allowed to be an absentee owner in this business?

45. What do the franchisees say about the franchisor, the product, the service, the training, the support, etc.? How many of the franchisees would re-invest in the franchise?

46. How many franchisees have failed and why?

47. How often has the franchisor been sued and why?

48. Does the franchisor have a solid financial statement?

49. What does the franchisor require of its franchisees? What does the franchisor promise to deliver to its franchisees?

50. When I'm ready to sell my franchise, or if circumstances (i.e., a death in the family, a better opportunity, etc.) force me to sell my franchise, what's involved in that process?

51. What is the tenure of the franchise agreement? If I want to renew my franchise, will I have to invest more money? Upgrade my location?

52. After reading the franchise disclosure document, do I feel comfortable with this franchise opportunity?

QUESTIONS TO ASK EXISTING FRANCHISEES . . .

The franchise disclosure document includes a list of current and previous franchisees. Use the list to contact franchisees by phone and in person. Some franchisees will welcome a personal visit – take advantage of those opportunities. Be sure to talk to the top franchisees in the network. If you can duplicate their experiences, you have a better chance of succeeding in the business. Bottom-rung franchisees are likely to be struggling and possibly failing. See if you can figure out what they're doing wrong or what to avoid if you become a franchisee.

53. Would you buy the same franchise again?

54. Do you trust the franchisor?

55. What's the franchisor's greatest strength? Greatest weakness?

56. If the president/CEO of the franchise company died, what then? How would the business continue?

57. How good is the franchisor's training and support?

58. How helpful is the operations manual? How often is it updated?

59. Do you get answers from the franchisor when you need them?

60. Have you renewed your franchise agreement or do you plan to?

61. Based on your experiences and those of other franchisees you know, how much money can I expect to make my first year as a franchisee? The third year? The fifth year?

62. What's the secret to the success of the top franchisees? Conversely, what are the bottom-rung franchisees doing wrong?

63. How much money do you spend to advertise and promote your business locally? Nationally?

64. What do you think about the quality of the company's products/services?

65. Is it difficult to attract and keep customers?

66. Do you attend the franchisor's regional and annual meetings? Why or why not?

67. I'd like to tell you about myself . . . and then would you tell me if you think my background, interests, and personality are a match for the franchise company?

68. What's the best way to make money with this business?

69. Who do you rely on most at the corporate office? Why?

70. Who should I avoid at the corporate office, or in the franchise network, and why?

71. Do you think the franchisor has the franchisees' best interests in mind?

72. How many franchisees have failed since you've joined the franchise network, and why?

73. Do you know any former franchisees who will speak to me about their experiences with the company?

74. Do you find the business as satisfying today as you did when you first got started?

75. If you were the franchisor, what would you change?

76. Is it challenging to find and keep employees?

77. What will be the biggest challenge I face as a franchisee?

78. Is your territory large enough? Too large? Too small? Is it a protected territory?

79. What keeps the franchisor from competing with you?

80. Can I visit you and spend a day watching what goes on in your business? Can I come to work for you . . . for example, could I work for you during a few weekends to get familiar with the business?

QUESTIONS TO ASK FORMER FRANCHISEES . . .

The franchise disclosure document must list names and contact information for franchisees who are no longer in the network, either because they chose not to renew their franchise agreement, they sold their business, their business failed, or the franchisor refused to renew their franchise agreement. Usually these people are not easy to locate and they don't want to speak to prospective franchisees. Existing franchisees will sometimes lead you to these individuals. Try your best to speak to former franchisees.

81. Why are you no longer part of the franchise network?

82. While you were a franchisee, what would you say were the company's strengths? Weaknesses?

83. Did you think you could trust the franchise company?

84. How did you relate to the other franchisees?

85. Can you give me some examples of how the company treated you fairly or unfairly?

86. If I decide to buy this franchise, what advice can you give me? What should I negotiate with the franchisor?

87. If you had the chance to operate your franchise again, what would you do differently?

QUESTIONS TO ASK YOUR
PROFESSIONAL ADVISORS...

I recommend that you consult with a franchise attorney (not just a business attorney) and a franchise-wise accountant (i.e., an accountant who is a franchisee or who is familiar with franchising and supports the concept). Some franchise brokers (i.e., sales representatives for franchise companies) will provide guidance and advice, but be careful. Franchise brokers have a vested interest – if you don't buy a franchise that they represent, they don't get paid.

88.   Is the franchise agreement fair for both parties? How is this franchise agreement different from other good franchise agreements that you have reviewed?

89.   If you were purchasing this franchise, what concessions, if any, would you ask for?

90.   What's your evaluation of the company's financial condition?

91.   Based on what you know about me and my situation, can I afford to invest in this franchise?

92.   Do you know the franchisor or any of the franchisees, and if so, how do you evaluate them and the franchise opportunity?

93.   Have I provided sufficient information for you to help

me evaluate this opportunity? What else, if anything, should I ask for from the franchisor?

94. Can you help me develop a business plan? When can I expect to break even? What kind of money can I earn from the business after two to three years?

95. If I need to borrow money, can you lead me to lenders? What's your opinion about converting my retirement fund into a loan for my business?

QUESTIONS TO ASK THE FRANCHISE COMPANY'S SUPPLIERS...

Most franchise prospects don't know that they can ask questions of suppliers – that is, companies that provide products and services to the franchise network. You will gain tremendous insights about the franchisor, the quality of the franchise network, the receptiveness to the company's product or service, etc., when you speak with suppliers! The same supplier (i.e., for beverages, snacks, paper goods, signage, uniforms, leases, etc.) may serve multiple franchise companies in the same industry.

96. Does the franchise company pay its bills on time?

97. Do you trust the franchise company?

98. Do you buy the company's products or use its services? Why or why not?

99. Why do some of the company's franchisees succeed while others fail?

100. If you were the franchisor, what would you do differently?

101. What do most of the franchisees complain about and why?

TIME FOR YOUR DECISION

Those are a lot of questions to ask, and once you start asking them and listening to the answers, you may come up with another 101 or more questions on your own. I hope you do, because asking questions is the best way to explore and evaluate franchise opportunities. Your homework may never have been more important than it is in evaluating franchises.

Of course, you can't ask questions forever – sooner or later the homework must be completed and you must set a date to graduate – or in this case, you must make a decision to buy or not buy a franchise.

If you decide not to buy a franchise because the answers to your questions didn't support any other decision, trust your decision. It's a good one. You will always have an opportunity to change your mind in the future, especially if you find that "perfect" franchise opportunity.

If you decide to buy a franchise, I hope you select a franchise that meets your needs and expectations and fulfills your dreams – thousands of people have done so already, and now I hope it's your turn.

Either way, if you ask enough questions of the right people, you are almost certain to make a good decision about buying or not buying a franchise.

BONUS QUESTION
ARE YOU A RISK TAKER?

When I interviewed franchisees for the book, *Franchising: The Inside Story howtobuyafranchise.com/theinsidestory/*, I asked them how they felt about taking risks. At the time, I thought franchisees were entrepreneurs and that entrepreneurs were risk takers. *And then I got an education!*

Franchisees may be (and they may think of themselves as) entrepreneurs, but they do not see themselves as risk takers. That explains why they buy franchises.

Risk takers put everything on the line with little or no assurance of a safety net. When they buy or develop a business, they invest their life savings and more (money borrowed from banks, family and friends). For the risk taker, it's do or die.

"Isn't that what franchisees do, too?" you may be asking (and good for you for asking questions!).

Not really. First of all, if the franchisee selected a franchise company with a good track record, one in which most of the franchisees have succeeded historically, the franchisee's safety net is the franchisor or the corporate office. The franchisor is responsible for providing the franchisee with a plan for operating the business, plus training and ongoing support. If a franchisee has a problem, he contacts the franchisor for help, and a good franchisor is responsive and effective.

Franchisees also serve as a safety net for challenged franchisees. A franchisee who can't figure out how to solve a business issue can always contact other franchisees within the network. "What did you do when you were faced with this problem?" Since franchisees of the same brand (i.e., McDonald's, Kwik Kopy, Signarama, Mr. Rooter, Pizza Inn, etc.) do not compete with each other, they willingly help each other.

Risk takers do not get the advantage of a safety net. It may be that they don't want one – the thrill is not in buying or building the business but in the risk. When risk takers encounter problems, they don't think about calling a friend in the same business, because they are competitors. Instead, risk takers try to figure it out on their own, and that often leads to failure.

Of course, there's still some risk in franchising. "I am a calculated risk taker," one prominent franchisee told me. "You can't be in business without taking some risks, it's the nature of business ownership. However, you don't have to be stupid about it. Or throw caution to the wind. You've got to realize that there's a downside to any business opportunity. So you invest cautiously. You do your homework, and franchising gives you that opportunity. You look around the corner, you think through the pros and cons, and you spend time talking to others who already own a franchise. So, no, I'm not a risk taker. But I take calculated risks as a franchisee."

Makes sense to me. How about you?

FAST-START TO YOUR FRANCHISE SUCCESS

These bullet points are a good reminder of how to use my list of questions as you explore franchising and specific franchise opportunities:

- Read the list of questions in its entirety and then go back and underline or highlight questions that you particularly want to ask.

- Create a list of people to interview . . . your list will include franchise specialists, franchisees, franchisors, and professional advisors.

- Interview yourself! Many of the questions on the list must be answered by you. Make sure you're a good fit, professionally and personally, for franchising. It's not for everyone.

- Schedule interviews. Keep in mind that you can interview people in person, by phone, via email, or other online services, such as Skype.

- Create a spreadsheet to record the answers you get to the questions you ask. The spreadsheet should include the questions, the name/affiliation of the person who responded, and the answers. Ultimately this spreadsheet will guide you as you make your decision to buy or not buy a franchise. By glancing at the spreadsheet, you will be able to quickly identify positive and negative responses.

- Create additional questions. As you ask questions, listen to the answers. The answers will often generate additional questions. Don't be afraid to ask them!

- Asking questions is one of the best ways to prepare yourself for the ultimate question that you must answer for yourself: *"Do I, or don't I, buy this franchise?"*

17 STEPS TO SUCCESSFULLY BUYING A FRANCHISE

Everything is possible with a system!

Outstanding achievements are the results of someone following a system. With the right systems, you can succeed at almost anything. What is it that you want? There's a system to help you get it.

You want to successfully buy a franchise? It won't surprise you, I don't think, to discover that there's a system for doing so. And here it is: *17 Steps to Successfully Buying a Franchise*. If you follow these guidelines, you're taking all the right steps to explore franchising, to consider the pros and cons of franchising, and, if franchising makes sense for you, to ultimately find a franchise opportunity worthy of your investment.

Even though I cannot guarantee your success as a franchisee – no one can because there are so many variables at play – if you complete these 17 steps, you can eventually sign your name to a franchise agreement with the confidence that you've done everything possible to ensure your own success as a franchisee. Of course, you must follow the system and complete each step with integrity.

Based on that understanding, here are 17 steps to successfully buying a franchise:

1. Educate Yourself

As you prepare to buy a franchise, spend time reading (or viewing informational videos) to make sure you understand what franchising is all about. You can also get good information at franchise conferences and through franchise advisors. One way or another, familiarize yourself with the fundamentals of franchising.

Questions you should ask:

- *Why is franchising so successful?*
- *What are the main reasons for franchise failure?*
- *How can I be sure that a franchisor is legitimate?*

2. Why Franchising Exists

Of all the points that you need to understand about franchising, the most important may be this: *Franchising is a system of distribution.* Franchising is a means for marketing and selling products and services. Don't get caught up in any of the hype about franchising. Yes, of course it's a way for you to own your own business, it may be the safest way to do so, and it may be your ticket to financial independence, but do not overlook the fundamental purpose of franchising: *It's to sell stuff!*

Questions you should ask:

- *Am I excited about distributing the franchisor's products and services?*
- *Do I see myself operating this system for five, 10, or more years?*

- *How can I be sure that the franchisor's system will work in my territory?*

3. Does Franchising Make Sense for You?

Be absolutely sure that franchising makes sense for you. Franchisors are not interested in selling franchises to the wrong prospects or investors. You should be equally as protective of yourself. Ask the question: *Is franchising for me?* Keep in mind that it's not for everyone. If it's not for you, don't force it. Read Part II of *Take the Fear Out of Franchising*. Utilize the DISC personality profile surveymonkey.com/r/howto-buyafranchise – it's free!

Questions you should ask:

- *What qualifies me to be a franchisee?*
- *Why do I want to be a franchisee?*
- *What type of franchise will make the most sense for me?*

4. Know Your Role as a Franchisee

Understand that the franchisor creates the *system* and the franchisees follow the system. Good franchisors know what needs to be done, day to day and month to month, to succeed in the business. And that's what they'll expect you to do. Everything you're required to do is part of the system, so you must be willing to follow it, even if you don't always agree with it. Otherwise, the franchisor can take away your franchise. The franchise agreement mandates that you follow the franchisor's system.

Questions you should ask:

- *How can I learn more about the franchisor's system?*
- *What aspects of the system may or may not be of interest to me?*
- *Do existing franchisees endorse the franchisor's system?*

5. You're Buying a License

By legal definition, a franchise is a license. A franchisor licenses a franchisee to operate a specific business in a specific manner at a specific location (or in a specific region) for a specific period of time. The license can be renewed and either party also can terminate it. Be sure you understand those details before you invest.

Furthermore, the franchisor retains ownership of (almost) everything! The franchisor's intellectual property, training materials, marketing methodologies, sales processes, possibly even phone numbers and clients, always remain the property of the franchisor and not the franchisee. These details will be explained in the Franchise Disclosure Document.

Questions you should ask:

- *What are the specific terms of the franchise agreement?*
- *Do I get a protected territory? (You may not want a protected territory and you do not necessarily need one, depending on the franchise.)*
- *What if I decide I want to sell the franchise; how do I do that?*

6. The Franchise Work Environment

Think about the franchise work environment. Most franchisors require franchisees to be owners/operators. In other words, you can't be an absentee owner. Some franchisors expect franchisees to work from home or a small office. Other franchisors require franchisees to work from a retail shop at a strip center or a mall. Other franchisors require franchisees to work from a van or another type of vehicle. In some cases, franchisees work alone; in other cases, franchisees manage employees. Once you know which work environment makes sense for you, pursue franchise opportunities that support your preferences.

Questions you should ask:

- *Do I want to manage people?*
- *Am I comfortable working alone, from my home or a small office?*
- *If I prefer one work environment but the franchise companies of my choice require a different work environment, can I adjust?*

7. Did You Know They Franchised THAT?

There are at least 75 primary industries that use franchising as their method of distribution. Once people explore franchises, they're surprised by the industries that have developed franchise opportunities It's best to find the industry that makes sense for you. Keep in mind that, from industry to industry, franchise investment costs vary.

Questions you should ask:

- *Which industries interest me the most?*
- *Which industries can I afford?*
- *Which industries provide me with the best opportunities?*

8. Look for the Right Opportunity

No one knows how many franchise opportunities exist, but estimates suggest there are 3,000 to 4,000 opportunities in North America alone. Many of these opportunities are local or regional, and some of the companies are sold out, so they're not offering franchises except internationally. Some industries include a dozen or more franchise companies offering similar and competitive franchise opportunities, while other industries may only include a handful of franchisors. Of course, these numbers are of little consequence considering that you're looking for just one franchise – the one that's best for you. You will find these opportunities by reading books and articles, attending expos, and by being observant: What's being franchised today that interests you?

Questions you should ask:

- *How much money can I invest in a franchise? The answer may dictate the industries that you should explore.*
- *How do I want to spend the next five, 10, or more years of my life in business?*
- *When it comes to "selling stuff," what excites me?*

9. Information is Free; Ask for It!

When you find a company that interests you, ask for

information. It's free, and it comes without any strings attached. Remember, a U.S.-based franchisor must provide U.S. citizens with a disclosure document at least two weeks before selling a franchise. The clock doesn't begin to tick until you acknowledge receiving the disclosure document. And franchisors will not send you that document until they've had an opportunity to speak with you and know that you are qualified to invest in their business. There's no reason not to ask for information, provided you're genuinely interested in the franchise. You can expect the company to ask you for your personal information before sharing information with you. Generally, a franchisor wants to get your email address, your phone number, the time frame in which you plan to buy a franchise, and an understanding of how much money you intend to invest in a business. By the way, it's a mistake to provide misleading information – once you're found out, do you think the franchisor will trust you?

Questions you should ask:

- *Are you planning to open franchises in my territory of choice?*
- *How much is the investment in your franchise?*
- *What makes your franchise business unique and amazing?*

10. Read the Information Carefully

Invest time to carefully read the information provided by the franchisor. Make sure you not only can see yourself as a franchisee but that you understand the business and the requirements of franchisees in your company of choice. The franchisor's preliminary information may not be specific, but the information in the franchisor's disclosure document must be specific. If you like what you're reading (perhaps even seeing, if the franchisor provides links to videos), plan to ask for the disclosure document.

Questions you should ask:

- *If I were to invest in this franchise, what else would I need to know?*
- *Is this a business that makes sense for my location or territory?*
- *Where's this business headed in the next five to 10 years?*

11. Attend the Franchisor's Discovery Day

Visit the franchisor. Almost every franchisor sponsors a Discovery Day. This is your chance to visit the franchisor's headquarters, meet company representatives (possibly even franchisees), and learn more about the franchise opportunity by listening to a variety of presentations and asking questions. The franchisor may also include a tour to show you the training center, the marketing department, etc. Franchisors do not charge a fee for Discovery Days, but you most likely will be expected to provide your own transportation and lodging. However, don't be afraid to ask the franchisor to pay for your expenses, or to share your expenses. Depending on how eager the franchisor is to sell a franchise, you may get a free trip. But even if you have to shell out some money for this experience, it's worth it. If you're married, the franchisor may want your spouse to attend, too.

Questions you should ask:

- *How is this business unique and amazing?*

- *How does this business compare to similar franchises?*
- *What's the future for this industry and this franchise in particular?*

12. Get Disclosed

Ask the franchisor for the Franchise Disclosure Document (FDD). Once the franchisor knows that you're a "serious" candidate to buy a franchise, by law the franchisor must "disclose" you before continuing to talk to you about the franchise opportunity. This is a very serious matter and franchisors are careful not to violate it.

When you ask for the disclosure document, the franchisor will ask you for detailed information to qualify your candidacy. Be prepared to tell the franchisor about your net worth, your personal and professional background (including any criminal violations), and the time frame in which you plan to buy a franchise. Expect the franchisor to investigate this information by running your credit history and a criminal background check. The franchisor may also require you to complete a franchise personality assessment.

Receiving a FDD does not obligate you to do anything! You must have this document for at least 14 days prior to buying the franchise. But you're not obligated until you sign the franchise agreement.

Questions you should ask:

- *How long has this franchise been in business; who owns it; how are the franchise company's executives qualified to be in their positions?*
- *How much training and support will I receive? Does it cost extra money?*

- *How often (if ever) have franchisees sued the franchisor, and why?*

13. Go to Work for a Franchisee

One of the most important steps you can take before buying a franchise is to talk to existing franchisees. Call them, visit them, and spend time with them. The FDD includes a list of existing and former franchisees – use that list; it's one of the most important tools for franchise exploration.

Existing franchisees will talk to you by phone, or if they're in close proximity to you, they may invite you to a personal meeting. Some franchisees may not be willing to talk to you at all, but most franchisees remember what it was like when they were exploring franchise opportunities, and they're willing to help you because someone once helped them. Franchisees also realize that it's important for their franchise networks to expand – it gives them greater visibility in the marketplace (more franchisees means more money in the national advertising fund) and greater clout when negotiating with suppliers.

Here's an idea that you will find extremely helpful: Go to work for an existing franchisee. Offer to work weekends or part time for a month or more to experience the franchise operation. This is a practical way for you to discover your interest in a specific business. Many franchisors will require that you at least meet with an existing franchisee to discuss your prospects for joining the franchise network.

"Are franchisees getting paid to tell me good things so that I'll buy the franchise?" If they are, the information will be revealed in the FDD or the franchisor is violating federal laws in the U.S.! Generally, franchisors do not pay franchisees for speaking to prospective franchisees. However, franchisors sometimes sponsor competitions (i.e., the franchisee who helps sell the most franchises in a year receives $10,000!). But that information also must be disclosed in the FDD.

Questions you should ask:

- *Would you buy this same franchise again?*
- *What are the franchisor's greatest strengths . . . weaknesses?*
- *How much money can I expect to earn after a year as a franchisee? After three years?*

14. Decide if You Can Afford the Investment

Study Item 7 of the franchisor's FDD to understand your financial commitment when you buy this franchise. Federal law requires U.S. franchisors to clearly disclose financial information in the FDD. Item 7, Estimated Initial Investment, presents each financial commitment in a chart that shows you when the money is due to be paid, to whom it must be paid (i.e. the franchisor, a media company, a landlord, or a supplier), and whether or not the money is refundable. This is the best way to see the required financial commitment at a glance.

Keep in mind that the franchisor must include every financial requirement in Item 7, which eliminates surprises. "Oh, we didn't tell you that you owe $5,000 for training?" That sort of thing doesn't happen anymore in franchising.

Questions you should ask:

- *Can I afford to invest this amount of money?*
- *Do existing franchisees say that the investment is reasonable?*

- *How does this financial commitment compare to investments in competitive opportunities?*

15. Understand the Ongoing Fees

Look at the ongoing royalty and advertising fee requirements, which are not part of Item 7. Most franchisors require franchisees to pay a percentage of gross sales as a royalty every month – the percentage may be as low as 5 percent and as high as 12 percent, and varies from company to company. The advertising fee is also a percentage of gross sales and may be in the range of 1 percent to 3 percent paid monthly.

Questions you should ask:

- *Do the royalty and advertising fees seem reasonable?*
- *How does the franchisor spend the royalty dollars paid by franchisees?*
- *Is the national advertising fund effective for boosting retail sales?*

16. Get Help!

Consult with your professional advisors. You should spend the money to engage a franchise attorney and an accountant prior to signing a franchise agreement. There are many franchise attorneys at work in the U.S. and other countries. You can find them through a franchise association, such as the International Franchise Association at Franchise. org. You will likely pay $500 to $1,500 for the attorney's basic services. You will likely pay more money to an attorney who does not specialize in franchise law – that's like asking your franchise attorney to handle a personal injury suit. If an attorney suggests he/she negotiate with the franchisor on your behalf, be very careful. Franchisors rarely negotiate and franchise attorneys know that. However, franchise attorneys also know areas in which a franchisor is likely to negotiate and may be helpful in that regard.

It's more difficult to find an accountant who is familiar with franchising and who understands franchising. Too often accountants are anti-franchising and they advise their clients to start businesses independently rather than to join a franchise network and pay fees. That's unfortunate because statistics demonstrate that, in many industries, franchises are more successful than independently owned businesses. My best advice for finding a "franchise friendly" accountant is to find an accountant who is also a franchisee! In other words, the accountant's practice is part of a franchise network. You can find these businesses through franchise associations. A good accountant will be able to help you develop a business plan and assess your financial risk, as well as rewards. Accounting fees vary widely, but for basic services, expect to pay $500 to $1,500. Keep in mind that you also may need an accountant after you become a franchisee to prepare your quarterly and annual statements.

Keep in mind that professional advisors are not supposed to make decisions for you. "Should I buy this franchise?" is a question that a good advisor will not answer. Advisors will point out pros and cons; ultimately, you make the decisions.

Other possible advisors include franchise brokers and coaches. When you engage these advisors, make certain that you understand what's in it for them. Brokers sell franchises for a living; they do not advise franchise prospects except as part of their mission to sell a franchise. Brokers generally do not charge fees to their clients because the franchisor pays them when they sell a franchise. There's nothing wrong with this arrangement, by the way, and franchisors who rely on brokers must reveal this information in the FDD.

Questions you should ask:

- *How does this franchise opportunity compare to others you've reviewed?*
- *What are the problem areas that you see investing in this type of franchise?*
- *Based on my financial situation, is this a franchise I can afford?*

17. Make Your Final Decision

Take a deep breath, offer up any final prayers, and say yes to the franchisor of your choice. Go ahead; sign the franchise agreement. Congratulations, you're a franchisee! If you did your homework and followed the recommendations offered to you in this book and through other sources, you're on your way to stardom!

Questions you should ask:

- *When does my training session begin?*
- *What three things must I be sure to do to succeed in this business?*
- *What three things must I be sure not to do to succeed in this business?*

When I'm buying a franchise, and when I coach my clients who are buying franchises, I use these 17 steps to success. Each step includes multiple tasks, and it's important to take the time to complete each step. If you have questions about how to complete these steps, or you need additional guidance, visit my blog at HowToBuyAFranchise.com and contact me.

FUNDING YOUR FRANCHISE ACQUISITION: WHERE DO YOU GET THE MONEY?

Two common mistakes that prospective franchisees make when they're exploring franchise opportunities are (1) ignorance of their personal financial status and capabilities; and (2) ignorance of the financial requirements to buy a franchise.

Do you know your credit score and how much cash you can invest in a franchise or bring to the table to leverage additional funds? Do you know what banks, leasing companies, the U.S Small Business Administration, and special funds designated for franchise lending will require of you to secure a loan?

The sooner you get on top of these issues the better – otherwise, you may be wasting your time. You should expect franchisors and franchise brokers to ask you these questions even before they give you a Franchise Disclosure Document. Not to do so could mean the franchisor is wasting time because you may not be financially qualified to acquire the franchise.

Good News for Borrowers

If you need to borrow money to acquire a franchise, the good news is that for the first time in many years you have multiple options available. While it was nearly impossible to borrow money to start a franchise between 2008 and 2010, opportunities are more plentiful today but still not what they were before the Great Recession.

While there's still not a national lender for franchise opportunities as existed prior to 2008, nowadays more community banks lend to franchisees, more franchisors lend to franchisees, several franchise-specific funds underwrite franchise acquisitions, and for those who have a retirement fund, the fund can be rolled into seed money to capitalize a business.

"Compared to what it was like before the recession, funding franchises is still difficult," explains Bob Coleman, editor of the Coleman Report, which provides information to bankers to help them make less risky small-business loans. "Lenders are scrutinizing deals and are particularly interested in the performance of the brand, something that didn't matter as much previously."

Not Good News for New Brands

"Unless a franchisor has 80 to 100 units, there's no deal," continues Coleman. "A startup brand and a new franchisee is not a favorable combination. Lenders want to see track records by both the brand and the franchisee. Lenders today know about unhappy franchisees and how to check for them, whereas (previously) they didn't care – [pay] 30 percent [money] down and you'd get the loan, but that doesn't happen anymore."

According to Coleman, lenders view franchises as "a little bit better risk than mom-and-pop businesses," but they're insisting on funding deals for established brands. They also prefer experienced franchisees. "If you've been successfully operating a unit for several years and now you need money to open another one to three units, you can get that money."

Franchising is Growing Once Again

As the economy continues to grow, lenders are becoming more receptive to franchise deals, and franchise companies are growing, too. In fact, Frandata, the franchise information firm based outside of Washington, D.C., reported that franchising is now growing at its fastest rate in five years, largely because prospective and existing franchisees have been able to find money to buy franchises.

How Do You Get a Loan Today?

So what's it going to take today to get the money you need to acquire a franchise opportunity?

Business financing expert Doug Smith of Biz Finance Solutions (bizfinancesolutions.com) in Colorado, explains that there are two types of funding: equity-based and debt-based.

"Using the money you have in your retirement plan, rolling it over without penalty or taxation, and using it as an injection to get a U.S. government-backed loan is equity financing," he says, and it's an option that many franchisees use today.

"Debt based funding requires a credit score and credit history to get a conventional bank loan or unsecured business financing, including equipment leasing, and unsecured personal loans. But if your credit score is weak or you've filed a bankruptcy, it's the kiss of death."

Your personal financial situation, and your thoughts about financial risk, may determine how you should proceed when you seek financing.

The 401(k) Rollover

Smith's preferred franchise funding strategy is the 401(k) Rollover, and most people don't seem to know about it. Or if they do, they've been told it's illegal or dangerous. However, this option has the blessing of the U.S. government.

Here are the facts you need to know:

If you have a retirement fund and you change employers, you have three important options:

1. Leave the fund where it is. The majority of people choose this option.

2. Move the fund into a new account, such as a self-directed IRA.

3. Move the fund to your new employer's 401(k), thus consolidating your retirement savings in one fund.

Most people aren't aware of Option #3, beginning with becoming your own employer!

That is, you can become a franchisee and establish a C Corporation with stock and a 401(k). Becoming your own employer puts you in the enviable position of self-funding your own business, tax-free! You can move – or what the Internal Revenue Service refers to as rollover – your existing retirement money into your new employer's 401k, and the cash can be used to buy and operate a franchise. It's tax-free, penalty-free (if done correctly), and it's legal. It may be your best option for funding your business, particularly if you don't have other resources, or you can't qualify for a traditional loan.

Isn't This Controversial?

The U.S. Internal Revenue Service and the Department of Labor have established guidelines and directives for implementing a 401(k) Rollover. You can't use the rollover to dodge taxes or to personally benefit from the money. Some years ago a financial broker was shut down for a period of time for stretching the rules, and that incident gave rise to the notion that the rollover is illegal. It's not. If you use the rollover for the right reasons – you can't use it for a scheme; it has to be used with a real business – you (or your advisor) set it up correctly and comply annually with the regulations, you should be able to avoid any objections or complications. Follow the spirit of the guidelines with appropriate intentions and you should remain in the clear.

Of course, the IRS reserves the right to change the rules, and that's why it's extremely important that you work with a credible company or broker that has a track record for successfully implementing and maintaining rollovers.

Two Benefits of a 401(k) Rollover

The 401(k) Rollover has made a good name for itself among franchisors, who frequently recommend the strategy to prospective franchisees.

Here are two reasons why:

If the franchise acquisition is a small investment – under $150,000 – franchisors know that lenders aren't attracted to small loans. There's no money to be made processing small loans, so lenders avoid them. That makes a rollover more attractive. Rollover money can be used to pay for the franchise fee and to buy equipment. When you don't have collateral – or you're buying a business that provides a service from your home, a vehicle, or a small office – the 401(k) Rollover may be your best choice for funding your business.

After a rollover, you can use the cash as equity to qualify for a conventional or SBA-guaranteed loan. You'll likely need a cash injection of 30 percent to secure a loan. In the past, borrowers used equity in real estate (i.e. their personal residence) to qualify for a loan. Now you can use rollover money for your cash injection.

"People who utilize a rollover are more successful in the average business," reveals Geoff Seiber, president and CEO of FranFund (franfund.com) in Fort Worth, Texas. "People who use this strategy tend to stay in business longer because they used their retirement money to fund their business and they don't have debt to service."

Can You Accept the Risks?

Used properly, the 401(k) Rollover is an aggressive way to capitalize your business. The challenge, however, is that by using it you give up the security of a retirement fund. Some people can't handle that emotionally. *Can you?* Will you feel comfortable knowing that your retirement money is now invested in your own business? If not, you probably don't want to use this funding strategy. On the other hand, people who start businesses and plan to operate them aren't usually looking for comfort.

In the U.S., numerous companies provide rollover services, including: Biz Finance Solutions, Guidant, FranFund, and Benetrends. Expect to spend about $5,000 with one of these firms to set up your rollover. The firm will also offer to provide necessary administrative services to keep your fund in check, and that may cost you about $100 monthly.

It's important to keep your rollover plan in compliance with the laws because the IRS audits these plans. "Under 2 percent of our plans are audited every year," says Seiber, "which is the norm in our industry. By not doing the administrative work properly, you're taking a bigger risk" if the IRS audits your account.

Unless you have a pile of cash that you intend to inject into your deal (i.e. a retirement fund that you will rollover or savings that you will bring to the table), your funding options are severely limited. It's even worse if you're a new franchisee and you want to buy a single unit – an existing franchisee with plans to expand or a multi-unit operator will find more options.

Look to Your Franchisor for Funding

Guys like Coleman, Smith, and Seiber are among a select corps of experts who can advise prospective franchisees when they need financing, but there's only so much they can do in a reticent financial market. If you can't take advantage of the programs they offer or recommend, your best source of funding may be your franchisor of choice. If you know that you will need money to acquire a franchise, look for franchisors who lend to franchisees. Even franchisors who don't loan money to franchisees know who will (and what's required), so ask your finance-related questions early in your franchise exploration.

And don't give up! Some of the most successful franchisees today started out by investing in a low-cost franchise and expanding when they could afford to do so. Many others started out with money borrowed from family and friends. If franchising makes sense for you, you'll find a franchise company that will help you clear the lending hurdles.

Here's One More Funding Option: VetFran

VetFran®, sponsored by the International Franchise Association (IFA) (www.franchise.org), helps veterans of the U.S. armed services buy franchise opportunities by providing financial assistance, training, and industry support.

VetFran was created by the late Don Dwyer Sr. –founder of The Dwyer Group, a conglomerate of franchise companies, to say "thank you" to America's veterans returning from the first Gulf War. After the Sept. 11, 2001 terrorist attacks, IFA re-launched VetFran and the program continues to this day.

Nearly 650 franchise brands voluntarily offer financial incentives and mentoring to prospective franchisees who are veterans. Thousands of veterans have utilized VetFran to buy franchises. If you're a veteran, be sure to ask your franchisor of choice, "Do you support VetFran?" This may be an additional source of funding for you.

FOREIGN INVESTORS: USE FRANCHISING TO GET A U.S. GREEN CARD

Foreign investors who want to move to the USA are taking advantage of the Immigrant Investor Program administered by the U.S. Citizenship and Immigration Services (USCIS). Applications are rising rapidly due to favorable changes in the program, and in part due to franchising.

Known as EB-5, the program was created to stimulate the U.S. economy through job creation and capital investment.

Here's how it works:

How the EB5 program works

A qualified foreigner invests $1-million directly into a business or into a regional fund that invests in businesses, including franchises of all types. If the investment creates at least 10 full-time jobs for at least two years, the investor gets a green card and eventually U.S. citizenship. In high unemployment areas, and rural areas, the investment is $500,000.

Foreign investors are using EB-5 to move their families to the U.S. or to send their children to the U.S. to study. A married investor gets visas for himself, his spouse, and all unmarried children under the age of 21.

Franchisors favor foreign operators

Foreigners operate many franchised businesses in the U.S. and franchisors welcome them because they are enthusiastic about learning a successful operating system that they and their family members can operate. However, EB-5 does not require investors to actually work in a business. As long as they fulfill the requirements of EB-5, the investors can live wherever they choose, start their own business, take a job, or retire in the U.S.!

As with any bureaucratic program, EB-5 takes time to complete. Investors must prove their money came from a lawful source and must also pass the scrutiny of U.S. immigration investors. The entire process may require a year before the investor and family can move to the U.S.

Direct and in-direct jobs count

Until recently, most EB-5 investors preferred real estate projects, but many of those investments failed to meet the job requirements. Franchising, on the other hand, is a much better choice. An injection of $1-million invested into certain franchised businesses can create upwards of 40 jobs. Consider, for example, a convenience store franchise. The franchise itself may need only 4 to 6 employees, but indirect jobs also count. A convenience store sells food and beverages and indirectly creates jobs to provide those products. Those indirect jobs count.

Franchisors are unaware of EB-5

Many franchise networks include multi-unit operators who seek expansion capital, and sometimes partners, to open a dozen or more units, or to expand into a new territory.

However, most franchisors don't know this program exists, so their multi-unit operators may not know, either.

The USCIS.com is a good place to learn more about this program.

FRANCHISE TERMS AND RESOURCES

The following lists provide information about franchising, including resources that may help you while you're pursuing a franchise opportunity. Please keep in mind that the inclusion of any resource does not imply the author's endorsement. The information in these lists is not exhaustive. If you're looking for something that you can't find in this section, please visit HowToBuyAFranchise.com and use our Contact form.

Franchise Terms

Here are some of the most common terms used in franchising.

Advertising Fee

Many franchise opportunities require franchisees to pay a monthly fee into an Advertising or Marketing Fund. The fee is generally represented as a percentage (for example, 2 percent) and is almost always calculated on the franchisee's gross sales, as opposed to net sales or profits. The Advertising Fee may also be a flat fee. The Advertising Fee is ongoing and will be collected while the franchise agreement is in effect. Advertising Fund monies are used to advertise the franchise brand, its products and/or services. This is not money to be used by the franchisor!

Ad Fund

Franchisees pay their Advertising Fees into an Ad Fund, which is used to underwrite the cost of advertising and promotions for franchisees. The franchisor, or Franchise Advisory Council, establishes the Ad Fund and oversees it on behalf of franchisees. Ad Fund money is often used to hire advertising and marketing agencies to assist the franchise network.

Disclosure

In some countries, and especially in the United States, franchisors are *required* by federal and some state laws to "disclose" individuals who are serious about acquiring a franchise. Disclosure is a process that includes providing prospective franchisees with a copy of the franchisor's Franchise Disclosure Document (FDD) and Franchise Agreement. The FDD must be delivered to a franchise candidate at least 14 days prior to the candidate purchasing the franchise. Disclosure minimizes fraudulent sales in franchising and promotes the safety and longevity of franchising. Franchisors are required to comply with specific disclosure regulations that disseminate helpful information to prospective franchisees in advance of paying any money or signing any documents.

Disclosure Document

See Franchise Disclosure Document.

Earning's Claim

An Earning's Claim (or a Financial Performance Representation) may be included in a franchisor's Franchise

Disclosure Document. An Earning's Claim documents the earnings of franchisees in the franchisor's network. *Most franchisors do not include Earning's Claims in their documents.* Those who do not are prohibited from making any oral or written statements concerning the actual or potential sales, costs, income or profits of their franchise opportunities.

Franchise

It's a license that grants an individual or an entity (i.e. a corporation) the right to use a franchisor's operating system for the purpose of marketing, selling and distributing the franchisor's products and/or services. A franchise is a license.

Franchise Agreement

A legal document (license) signed by both the franchisor and the franchisee granting the franchisee the right to operate the franchise system for a specified period of time, in a specified format, and sometimes in a specified location. It's the legally binding document between franchisor and franchisee.

Franchise Associations

There are approximately 40 trade associations throughout the world that represent the interests of franchisors and franchisees. See International Franchise Association.

Franchise Disclosure Document

Every franchisor in the United States is required to complete and maintain a Franchise Disclosure Document (FDD). The FDD, in layperson's language, describes the franchise opportunity. The items of disclosure are standard for all franchise companies. There are 23 Items that require disclosure, including Litigation, Initial Franchise Fee, Franchisee's Obligations, Franchisor's Obligations, Territory, Restrictions On What The Franchisee May Sell, Renewal, Termination, Transfer and Dispute Resolution, List of Outlets (Franchisees), Financial Statements, and more. Prospective franchisees should read the FDD several times before investing in the franchise.

Franchisee

The individual or entity (i.e. a corporation) that's assigned the rights to a franchise by a franchisor.

Franchise Expo

Franchise companies come together under one roof to exhibit their franchise opportunities for a day or more. The public is invited to these events. Expos sometimes include educational programs.

Franchise Fee

A one-time, upfront fee required by the franchisor. It must be disclosed in the Franchise Disclosure Document.

Franchise Portal

A website that promotes franchise opportunities and may also include educational information about franchising. The best example: FranchiseExpo.com.

Franchisor

The company that grants franchises to franchisees. The franchisor controls and owns the franchise system.

International Franchise Association

IFA is the world's largest trade organization representing both franchisors and franchisees. Headquarters: Washington, D.C. Website: franchise.org.

International Franchise Expo

The world's premier event among franchise expos is sponsored by the International Franchise Association. The producer of the IFE is MFVExpositions. Website: ifeinfo.com.

Royalty Fee

A payment of money by the franchisee to the franchisor. Usually represented as a percentage (as an example, 6 percent) and paid weekly or monthly. May also be a flat weekly or monthly fee. Royalties are almost always paid on the franchisee's gross sales, as opposed to net sales or profits. This is an ongoing fee that must be paid during the period of time the franchise agreement/license is in effect. The royalty fee must be disclosed in the Franchise Disclosure Document.

FRANCHISE RESOURCES

FRANCHISE ASSOCIATIONS

International Franchise Association

1900 K St., NW, Suite 700
Washington, DC 20006
Phone: (202) 628-8000
Website: franchise.org

In addition to representing franchisors and franchisees, the IFA also represents the Council of Franchise Suppliers, which includes attorneys, accountants, consultants, franchise brokers, and others who may be able to assist you in your exploration of franchising. IFA promotes numerous books and other resources about franchising and publishes *Franchising World* magazine. Free resources are included on the IFA's website.

Canadian Franchise Association

5399 Eglinton Ave. West, Suite 116
Toronto, Ontario
Canada M9C 5K6
Telephone: 416-695-2896
Email: info@cfa.ca

Website: cfa.ca
For a list of Franchise Associations Worldwide:
www.franchise.org

FRANCHISE EXPOSITIONS

MFV Expositions
Telephone: 201-226-1130
Website: mfvexpo.com

In addition to the International Franchise Expo, MFV Expositions produces the West Coast Franchise Expo, Franchise Expo South and international franchise events including *Feria Internacional de Franquicias* in Mexico City.

U.S. GOVERNMENT RESOURCES

U.S. Small Business Administration: www.sba.gov
U.S. Commerce Department International Trade Administration: ita.doc.gov

BOOKS, PERIODICALS & PORTALS

7 Dirty Little Secrets of Franchising: Protect Your Franchise Investment, Amazon.com

12 Amazing Franchise Opportunities for 2015, Amazon.com

101 Questions to Ask Before You Invest in a Franchise, Amazon.com

Bond's Franchise Guide, Amazon.com

Buy "Hot" Franchises Without Getting Burned, Amazon.com

Entrepreneur, entrepreneur.com, publishes the Franchise 500 every January

Franchise Handbook, franchisehandbook.com

FranchiseExpo.com franchiseexpo.com

FranchiseGator.com franchisegator.com

Franchise Opportunities Guide, franchise.org

Franchise Times, franchisetimes.com

Franchise Update, franchise-update.com

Franchising World, franchise.org

AUTHOR'S BIOGRAPHY

John P. Hayes, Ph.D., began working in the franchise community in 1979 as a freelance writer. He continues to write about franchising for media worldwide, including newspapers, magazines and books. On several occasions he has been a franchisee, and for several years he served as the President  & CEO of one of America's major franchise companies, HomeVestors of America, Inc. He is one of the few people to have been a franchisee, a franchisor, and an advisor to franchisors and franchisees.

For many years John's client list included the International Franchise Association (IFA), the International Franchise Expo (IFE), and dozens of franchise companies. For several years he toured the U.S. as a part of IFA's regional training faculty, and on many occasions he has been a speaker and trainer for IFA, the IFE, and countless franchise companies. For several years starting in 1989, he traveled with the IFA's international franchise trade missions, marketing U.S. franchise opportunities in Europe, South America, the Pacific Rim, and the Far East.

John is a frequent speaker at international franchise expos and a guest on radio and television to discuss franchise topics. He was featured in a 30-minute television infomercial called *The Power of Franchising*. Through the years he has assisted franchisors and franchisees internationally to sell or acquire master licensing rights. For nearly 30 years he has taught the most popular symposium at the International Franchise Expo: The A to Zs of Buying a Franchise.

He is the co-author of **Franchising: The Inside Story** (with franchisor John Kinch); **You Can't Teach a Kid to Ride a Bike at a Seminar** (with franchisor David Sandler); **Start Small, Finish Big, 15 Lessons to Start & Operate Your Own Business** (with the co-founder of Subway); and **Network Marketing for Dummies** (with Zig Ziglar).

Your Personal Franchise Coach:
Dr. John P. Hayes

Schedule private, one-on-one coaching sessions with franchise and business-building expert, Dr. John Hayes. See www.howtobuyafranchise.com.

Coaching especially for:

Prospective Franchisees

Existing Franchisees

Startup Franchisors

Startup businesses

Partnerships

Family Businesses

Network Marketers

You select the topics to discuss, including:

Buying a franchise; becoming a franchisee

Are you the right fit for becoming a franchisor or franchisee?

Capturing and keeping the right customers in your business

How to sell franchises (domestically, internationally)

Developing a Franchise Advisory Council

Marketing Master Licenses internationally

Building your Leadership Team to manage your business

Working "on" your business and not always "in" your business

Developing training and support systems for your franchisees

Improving the franchisor/franchisee relationship

Creating an Ops program that benefits franchisor and franchisees

Writing a book to promote your business

Other topics of your choice

Message to Prospective Franchisees:

I do not sell franchises and I am not a broker for any franchise concept. First and foremost, I will help you determine if franchising makes sense for you. If it doesn't, save your time, save your money, and move on.

If franchising makes sense for you, I'll help you explore the type of franchise that would be best suited to your interests, skills, values and economic situation. As you conduct your due diligence (in part by asking/answering the questions in *101 Questions to Ask Before You Invest in a Franchise*), I'll look over your shoulder and guide you along the way. You can rely on me to help you walk through the minefield of franchise discovery. Along the way I'll introduce you to professionals (i.e. accountants, attorneys, brokers, advisors) who can assist you as you acquire a franchise.

Choose One Session or Multiple Sessions

Whether you need just one session or you want to schedule weekly sessions, the choice is yours.

Discounts are available for more than three sessions. You may include partners or other members of your corporate team on the same coaching call for one fee. Details available at howtobuyafranchise.com.

BizComPress

Do you have a story to tell that will help others improve their life, their business, or otherwise make a difference? BizComPress can help you reach the widest audience possible. Founded by authors for authors, BizComPress is a new kind of publishing company. Our award-winning team will help you write your book, edit it, design it, publish it, and promote it. And you keep the majority of your earnings!

Whether you already have a manuscript, or just the seed of an idea, contact us and we'll provide honest feedback based on decades of experience in book publishing. If we think the manuscript or the idea has a market, we can develop a plan that fits your budget. You'll be on your way to becoming a published author.

For more information contact Scott White at 214-458-5751 or contact Scott via BizComPress.

ONE LAST THING

I'll be very grateful if you will take a few moments and share your thoughts about this book. Log in to your Amazon.com account and please write a review for *How To Buy A Franchise Collection Volume I.* Your review can be as brief or as detailed as you prefer. Thank you!

Made in the USA
Columbia, SC
17 August 2023

21778000R00075